RECKLESS Reptiles

Alix Wood

Gareth Stevens PUBLISHING

Please visit our website, www.garethstevens.com. For a free color catalog of all our high-quality books, call toll free 1-800-542-2595 or fax 1-877-542-2596.

Cataloging-in-Publication Data
Names: Wood, Alix.
Title: Reckless reptiles / Alix Wood.
Description: Buffalo, NY : Gareth Stevens Publishing, 2027. | Series: Nature's worst parents | Includes glossary and index.
Identifiers: ISBN 9781482477740 (pbk.) | ISBN 9781482477757 (library bound) | ISBN 9781482477764 (ebook)
Subjects: LCSH: Reptiles--Juvenile literature.
Classification: LCC QL644.2 W65 2027 | DDC 597.9--dc23

Published in 2027 by
Gareth Stevens Publishing
2544 Clinton St.
Buffalo, NY 14224

Designed and written by Alix Wood

Picture Credits: all illustrations © Alix Wood;

Photo credits — cover (except top left), 5, 6 bottom, 7, 8, 9, 11, 12 main image, 15, 16, 19, 22, 23 bottom, 24, 26, 29, 31 © Adobe Stock Images; 6 top © Danadi Sutjianto/Creative Commons; 12 inset © Louisvdw/Creative Commons; 18 inset © Geoff Gallice/Creative Commons; 20 © Hilary Jeffkins/Naturepl.com; 23 top © Steve Jurvetson/Creative Commons; 27 © Salamandra 2021/Creative Commons; 28 © John Mather/Creative Commons, 30 top © Brandon Antonio Segura Torres & Priscilla Vieto Bonilla/Creative Commons; 30 bottom © André Karwath/Creative Commons

Printed in China
CPSIA compliance information: Batch #QS27GS: For further information contact Gareth Stevens at 1-800-542-2595.

Find us on

Contents

WHAT ARE REPTILES AND AMPHIBIANS?

Reptiles and amphibians usually live in warm, damp places such as wetlands, forests, and grasslands. They are cold-blooded. That means they cannot make their own body heat to stay warm. Reptiles and amphibians both have backbones.

Reptiles

Most reptiles are covered in dry, scaly skin. They can be found in water and on the land. Nearly all reptiles lay eggs with tough shells.

Some reptiles have four legs, and some have no legs.

Amphibians

Amphibians don't have scaly skin. Their larvae hatch from eggs laid in the water. Larvae breathe like a fish, using **gills**. As they grow, they develop **lungs** and can spend time on land.

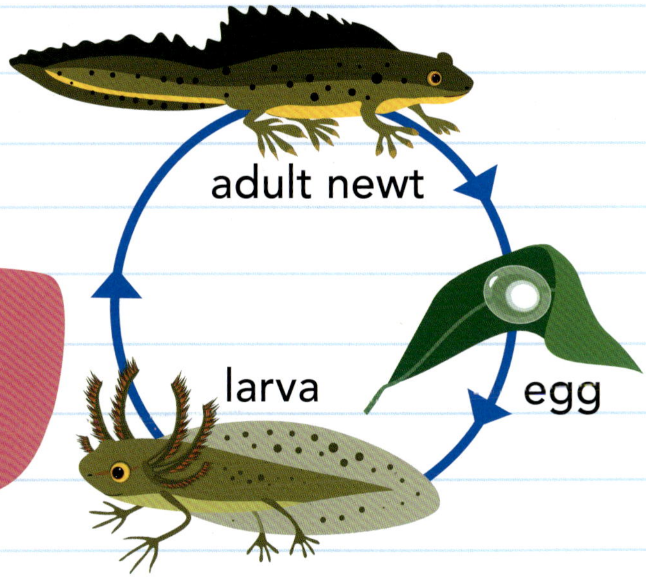

This change that amphibians go through is called metamorphosis.

a heron eating a baby sea turtle

Most reptiles and amphibians are terrible parents! The moms lay their eggs, cover them up, and forget about them. **Predators** often eat most of their babies.

SOME reptiles and amphibians are great parents, but most of them are pretty awful!

Komodo Dragons

These fierce lizards can be 10 feet (3 m) long and weigh as much as an adult man. The mom buries her eggs underground. The young Komodo dragons hatch around eight months later.

Do these huge lizards guard their babies from predators? Not a chance!

THE KIDS BETTER RUN IF I'M HUNGRY!

Newly-hatched Komodo dragons rush up the nearest tree to hide. Their parents don't protect them. In fact, they eat them!

a young komodo dragon hiding in a tree

Why Do They Do That?

The parents are hungry! Baby dragons make up 10 percent of their diet!

Komodo dragons can swallow a goat whole! Their blood-red saliva helps them swallow. It takes around 20 minutes to swallow a goat. They sometimes ram their snack against a tree to force it down their throat!

WHAT?

Young Komodo dragons roll in poop or dead animal guts to try to keep the adults from eating them!

Hognose Snakes

Most snakes aren't great parents. The moms just lay their eggs and slither away. Baby snakes have to look out for themselves. Some snakes don't lay eggs. The moms give birth to live, tiny snakes. These moms may stay and protect their babies for a few days.

A hognose snake lays eggs, but mom sticks around for a while too...For a snack!

After some of the hognose snakes have hatched, mom may eat any unhatched eggs. She also eats any dead baby snakes.

WHAT?

Snakes that eat other snakes will see any egg or snake as food. They don't care that they might be family!

Why Do They Do That?

Laying eggs uses up a lot of energy. So mom needs a snack! Scientists believe snakes may only eat the eggs and babies that have something wrong with them and won't survive.

Leopard Tree Iguanas

These South American iguanas live together in colonies. Unusually for iguanas, instead of laying eggs, they give birth to live young.

The iguana mom has between two and four babies in the spring. Mom stays in the underground nest with her babies for a day or two. Then, she seals up the entrances to the nest, with her babies still inside, and leaves.

WHAT?

Mom does leave her babies with a snack to keep them going, though. It's some of her poop!

Why Do They Do That?

Mom's poop is actually a **nutrient-filled** treat for the baby iguanas! The poop also gives them special **bacteria**, which helps them digest the plants they will eat once they leave the nest.

I GIVE MY BABIES A SNACK—OF POOP!

The poop's smell helps the young iguanas recognize their mom once they dig their way out of the nest.

Tortoises

All turtles are terrible parents! Tortoise moms lay their eggs, bury them, and then walk away. Tortoise parents have NOTHING to do with their kids.

Tortoise moms do dig their nests in a good place, at least. They choose a sunny slope with loose soil. The slope stays warm and dry. The soil makes it easy for the kids to dig their way out.

laying eggs in a nest

WHAT?

If the nest temperature isn't quite right, the eggs won't hatch. Even if the temperature is perfect, only four percent of **hatchlings** survive once they dig their way to the surface.

Weirdly, warm nest temperatures produce more girl tortoises. Cold temperatures produce more boys.

Why Do They Do That?

The tortoises' strange parenting works for them. If the parents stayed near the nest, their scent might attract egg-eating predators. Also, adult tortoises are big and heavy. They may accidentally crush the eggs. The hatchlings may be better alone. They are born knowing how to find food and hide from predators.

Darwin's Frogs

Female Darwin's frogs lay their eggs in the damp forest soil. Then, they hop away and leave the rest of the care to dad.

As soon as dad spots movement inside the eggs, he gulps them down! Dad doesn't eat them, though. He carefully holds the eggs in his mouth.

The dad frog may not eat for weeks while the baby frogs are in his mouth.

I SWALLOW MOM'S EGGS!

WHAT?

The frog's eggs hatch into tadpoles inside the dad's mouth. The tadpoles survive by eating their egg sac and special food that comes from the walls of dad's mouth. After around six weeks, the tadpoles turn into tiny frogs.

Once the tadpoles have turned into frogs, dad coughs them up!

Why Do They Do That?

It may seem gross, but dad's mouth is a very safe place to be for the tiny tadpoles. Once they have grown into frogs, they have a much better chance of survival.

If a Darwin's frog feels threatened, it does something very weird to defend itself! It flips onto its back and pretends to be a dead leaf!

Long-Tailed Skinks

A skink is a type of lizard. Like most lizards, they are not the best parents. These skinks, at least, try to find a safe place for their nest. The female lays up to 16 oval eggs in holes or under rocks or buildings.

The skink parents guard their nest from predators too. So far, so good.

IF MY EGGS ARE IN DANGER, I EAT THEM!

skink eggs

WHAT?

Egg-eating snakes attack skink nests. The skink mom will try to fight off the predator. But, if it looks as though the snake will win, the mom will eat her own eggs instead.

Why Do They Do That?

Eating your own eggs may seem pretty weird, but the skink mom has a good reason to do what she does.

When mom realizes the snake is winning, she knows she will lose her eggs. So, she figures eating them herself will make her strong enough to lay more. And the snake will get weaker since it won't get a good meal.

Glass Frogs

Weird, see-through bodies give these tiny glass frogs their name. If you look closely, you can see their heart beating! Their transparent skin helps them hide in their surroundings.

The mom glass frog lays her eggs on a leaf above a stream. She needs to keep the eggs damp or they will dry out. So, she has come up with a strange solution!

WHAT?

The mom glass frog drinks water through her skin. Then she pees on the eggs to keep them moist.

When the wiggly tadpoles hatch, they fall into the stream below.

Seriously, Mom?!

Why Do They Do That?

The eggs are safer from predators on their leaf. But if the eggs dry out they won't hatch into tadpoles. Mom needs to keep them damp! The fall may be scary, but the tadpoles quickly find water!

Caecilians

Caecilians are a type of blind, worm-like amphibian. They live underground in soil or in riverbeds. Most caecilians moms are great, but one type feeds their kids something pretty gross.

I GET THE KIDS TO EAT MY SKIN!

The babies feast on mom's outer layer of skin every three days. This gives mom time to grow a new layer before their next meal.

Why Do They Do That?

Mom's skin is full of nutrients. The hungry baby caecilians grow 10 times larger in one week after eating the skin. Mom's skin is also full of helpful **microbes**. These microbes help keep the caecilians healthy.

The babies' special teeth lift small pieces of skin, so they don't really harm their mom.

There is a type of caecilian whose moms produce a white fluid, a little like milk, for their babies to drink.

WHAT?

Some caecilians don't lay eggs. They give birth to live young. These young caecilians start eating their mom's insides before they are born!

Olive Ridley Sea Turtles

Like most reptiles, sea turtle moms and dads don't stick around to care for their babies. The mom digs a hole, buries her eggs in the sand, and leaves them.

digging a nest

Why Do They Do That?

The mother turtles return to the beach where they were born to lay their eggs. They made it to adulthood, so there is a good chance their babies will too. The mom hides her eggs well. The soft sand protects them and keeps them warm until the turtles hatch.

The turtles have a special tooth that helps them break out of the egg.

The newly-hatched turtles dig their way out of the nest and run.

MY KIDS BETTER RUN FOR THEIR LIVES!

WHAT?

The tiny turtles all hatch at once. They have to run across a beach full of predators to reach the ocean. Crabs, birds, raccoons, and foxes all snack on the turtles. Over 90 percent get eaten!

Crocodiles

Crocodiles are large, terrifying reptiles. Males can be 20 feet (6 m) long and weigh as much as a car. They have thick, plated skin and very sharp teeth.

A crocodile's powerful jaws have a bite twice as strong as a lion's!

So, how do you think crocodiles carry their tiny babies?

Baby crocodiles are less than a foot (30 cm) long when they hatch.

Why Do They Do That?

The safest way for baby crocodiles to travel is to hitch a ride in mom's mouth. No predator would risk going near them! The mom holds them very carefully. A stretchy pouch under her chin means she can carry several babies at once.

Crocodiles are actually good parents. Mom guards her nest until the babies are ready to hatch. She helps uncover the eggs and sometimes helps open the eggs using her tongue.

WHAT?

Mom has to protect her babies from other crocodiles. Adult crocodiles think babies are a tasty snack.

Japanese Giant Salamanders

These strange, huge salamanders can grow to the size of a park bench. They are covered in warts, with tiny eyes and a mouth as wide as their head! In late summer, male salamanders search for underwater burrows. There aren't many good nest places, so the males fight over the best ones.

Salamander dads guard their dens. Only females are allowed in to lay their eggs.

Once mom lays her eggs, she leaves, and dad takes over. Dad fans his tail over the eggs to create bubbles of air. He turns each egg to keep the yolk from sticking to the sides too.

DAD'S GREAT— WITH SOME OF THE EGGS!

WHAT?

The salamander dad eats some of the eggs!

Why Do They Do That?

Scientists think dad only eats the eggs that have either failed to thrive or are moldy. Eating those eggs helps the rest of the eggs stay healthy. Moldy eggs pollute the water.

Labord's Chameleons

Labord's chameleons live on the island of Madagascar. Its western forests have a very dry season and a very wet season.

The chameleons can't find enough food in the dry season. So, every single Labord's chameleon dies.

Are Labord's chameleons extinct? No, the eggs mom laid are safe underground, waiting to hatch.

WHAT?

Their short life means these chameleons have to race to find a mate. The males often kill each other fighting over a female. The female uses the last of her energy to lay her eggs.

When the baby chameleons hatch, they are on their own. There is not a single adult chameleon left alive to help them.

Why Do They Do That?

With no food around, Labord's chameleons only live for around four months. Their eggs take up to nine months to develop. But mom and dad have done all they can to make sure their species survives.

Glossary

bacteria seen under a microscope

bacteria Tiny living things made of only one cell. Bad bacteria can cause sickness. Good bacteria can help us digest food.

gills Special body parts that help animals, like this newt larva, breathe underwater.

hatchlings Baby birds or other animals that have just hatched from their eggs.

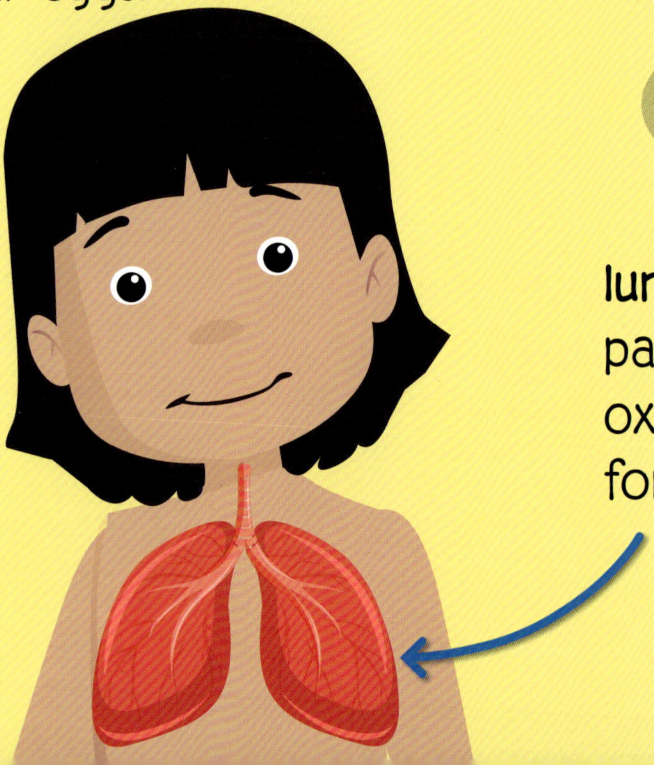

lungs Bag-like body parts that fill with oxygen and are used for breathing.

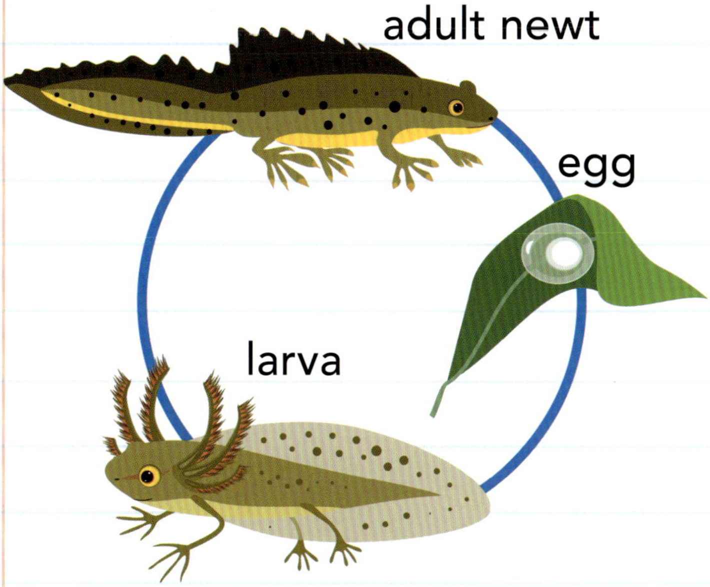

metamorphosis When a living thing changes form dramatically as it becomes an adult, such as a larva becoming a newt.

microbes Tiny living things, which can cause disease.

nutrients Something in food that helps people, animals, and plants live and grow.

predators An animal that hunts and eats other animals for food.

Index